MW00825132

HOLT

Civics

HOLT, RINEHART AND WINSTON
A Harcourt Education Company

Austin • Orlando • Chicago • New York • Toronto • London • San Diego

Contents

Guided Reading Strategies

UNIT 1 A TRADITION OF DEMOCRACY

CHAPTER 1 We the People
1.1 Civics in Our Lives 1
1.2 Who Are U.S. Citizens? 2
1.3 The American People Today 3

CHAPTER 2 Foundations of Government
2.1 Why Americans Have Governments 4
2.2 The First U.S. Government 5
2.3 A New Constitution 6

CHAPTER 3 The U.S. Constitution
3.1 Ideals of the Constitution 7
3.2 The Three Branches of Government 8
3.3 A Flexible Document 9

CHAPTER 4 Rights and Responsibilities
4.1 The Bill of Rights 10
4.2 Guaranteeing Other Rights 11
4.3 Citizens' Duties and Responsibilities 12

UNIT 2 THE FEDERAL GOVERNMENT

CHAPTER 5 The Legislative Branch
5.1 The Senate and the House of Representatives 13
5.2 How Congress Is Organized 14
5.3 The Powers of Congress 15
5.4 How a Bill Becomes a Law 16

CHAPTER 6 The Executive Branch
6.1 The Presidency 17
6.2 Powers and Roles of the President 18
6.3 Executive Departments and the Cabinet 19
6.4 Independent Agencies and Regulatory Commissions 20

CHAPTER 7 The Judicial Branch
7.1 Equal Justice under the Law 21
7.2 The Federal Court System 22
7.3 The Supreme Court 23

UNIT 3 STATE AND LOCAL GOVERNMENT

CHAPTER 8 State Government
8.1 The States 24
8.2 State Legislatures 25
8.3 The State Executive Branch 26
8.4 State Courts 27

CHAPTER 9 Local Government
9.1 Units of Local Government 28
9.2 Town, Township, and Village Governments 29
9.3 City Government 30
9.4 How Governments Work Together 31

UNIT 4 THE CITIZEN IN GOVERNMENT

CHAPTER 10 Electing Leaders
10.1 A Two-Party System 32
10.2 Political Party Organization 33
10.3 The Right to Vote 34
10.4 Nominating and Electing Our Leaders 35

CHAPTER 11 The Political System
11.1 Shaping Public Opinion 36
11.2 Interest Groups 37
11.3 Taking Part in Government 38

CHAPTER 12 Paying for Government
12.1 Raising Money 39
12.2 Types of Taxes 40
12.3 Managing the Country's Money 41

UNIT 5 THE CITIZEN IN SOCIETY

CHAPTER 13 Citizenship and the Family
13.1 The Changing Family 42
13.2 Law and the Family 43
13.3 Your Family and You 44

CHAPTER 14 Citizenship in School
14.1 The U.S. School System 45
14.2 The Best Education for You 46
14.3 Developing Your Life Skills 47

CHAPTER 15 Citizenship in the Community
15.1 Kinds of Communities 48
15.2 Purposes of Communities 49
15.3 Citizens Serve Communities 50

CHAPTER 16 Citizenship and the Law
16.1 Crime in the United States 51
16.2 The Criminal Justice System 52
16.3 Juvenile Crime 53

UNIT 6 THE AMERICAN ECONOMY

CHAPTER 17 The Economic System
17.1 The Economic System at Work 54
17.2 Business Organizations 55
17.3 Making Business Decisions 56

CHAPTER 18 Goods and Services
18.1 American Production 57
18.2 Distributing Goods 58
18.3 You the Consumer 59

CHAPTER 19 Managing Money
19.1 Money and Credit 60
19.2 Banks and Banking 61
19.3 Saving and Investing 62
19.4 Insurance against Hardship 63

CHAPTER 20 Economic Challenges

20.1 The Business Cycle 64
20.2 Coping with Economic Challenges 65
20.3 Labor and Management 66

CHAPTER 21 The U.S. Economy and the World

21.1 Overview of the US. Economy 67
21.2 Factors Affecting the U.S. Economy 68
21.3 Government's Role in the U.S. Economy 69
21.4 Living in a World Economy 70

CHAPTER 22 Career Choices

22.1 The Challenge of a Career 71
22.2 The World of Work 72
22.3 Unlimited Opportunities 73
22.4 Learning More about Careers 74
22.5 Learning More about Yourself 75

UNIT 7 THE UNITED STATES AND THE WORLD

CHAPTER 23 Foreign Policy

23.1 Conducting Foreign Relations 76
23.2 Working for Peace 77
23.3 The United Nations 78

CHAPTER 24 Charting a Course

24.1 Development of U.S. Foreign Policy 79
24.2 The Cold War 80
24.3 New Trends 81

UNIT 8 MEETING FUTURE CHALLENGES

CHAPTER 25 Improving Life for All Americans

25.1 Improving Communities 82
25.2 Ensuring Rights for All 83
25.3 Protecting Citizens' Health and Safety 84

CHAPTER 26 The Global Environment

26.1 Understanding Ecology 85
26.2 Pollution 86
26.3 Energy Resources 87
26.4 Our Future on Earth 88

CHAPTER  1   Guided Reading Strategies 1.1

We the People

READING THE SECTION As you read this section, fill in the term that matches the following definitions or descriptions.

_____   **1.** The hope of a better life for everyone

_____   **2.** Legally recognized member of a country

_____   **3.** Organizations, institutions, and individuals who exercise authority as a political unit over a group of people

_____   **4.** Ideals the U.S. government and American way of life are based on

_____   **5.** They rule through their elected officials.

_____   **6.** The study of what it means to be a U.S. citizen

POST-READING QUICK CHECK After reading the section, list the 10 characteristics of good citizens in the spaces below.

1. _____

2. _____

3. _____

4. _____

5. _____

6. _____

7. _____

8. _____

9. _____

10. _____

Name _____ Class _____ Date _____

READING THE SECTION As you read the section, match each term with the correct definition. Write the letter of the definition on the answer line.

_____ **1.** immigrants

_____ **2.** archaeologists

_____ **3.** quotas

_____ **4.** aliens

_____ **5.** refugees

_____ **6.** native-born citizen

_____ **7.** deport

_____ **8.** naturalization

a. Numbers of immigrants that can come from a country or region

b. Person born in any U.S. state or territory

c. People fleeing persecution in their homeland

d. People in the United States who are citizens of another country

e. Scientists who study the remains of past cultures

f. To force a person to leave a country

g. Legal process by which an alien may become a citizen

h. People who come to this country from other lands

POST-READING QUICK CHECK After reading the section, describe the naturalization process, or the steps by which an alien may become a U.S. citizen.

_____

_____

_____

_____

_____

_____

_____

_____

CHAPTER **1**

Guided Reading Strategies 1.3

We the People

READING THE SECTION As you read the section, complete each sentence below by writing the appropriate word or phrase in the space provided.

1. The main purpose of a(n) _____ is to find the size of each state's population.

2. The number of Americans living in _____ has continued to increase while the number of Americans living in _____ has decreased.

3. People who live in the _____ now outnumber those living in cities.

4. Areas made up of cities and their suburbs are called _____.

5. Because of the _____ to warmer climates, states in the South and West, known as the _____, have experienced rapid population growth.

6. The introduction of the _____ made it possible for people to travel longer distances to work.

7. The three largest minority groups in the United States are

_____, followed by _____ and

_____.

8. Today the traditional family accounts for less than _____ percent of U.S. households.

9. _____ percent of married women are in the U.S. workforce.

10. The current average life expectancy in the United States is approximately

_____.

POST-READING QUICK CHECK After you have finished reading this section, list the six cities that lie in the Sunbelt that are among the 10 most populous in the United States.

1. _____   **4.** _____

2. _____   **5.** _____

3. _____   **6.** _____

 **CHAPTER 2**   Guided Reading Strategies 2.1

Foundations of Government

READING THE SECTION As you read the section, complete each sentence by writing the correct letter in the space provided.

_____ **1.** A government controlled by a king or queen is a
   a. dictatorship.
   b. monarchy.
   c. totalitarian government.
   d. democracy.

_____ **2.** A government in which one person holds all the power is a
   a. dictatorship.
   b. monarchy.
   c. oligarchy
   d. democracy.

_____ **3.** In a(n) _____ system, rulers do not answer to the people.
   a. republic
   b. representative democracy
   c. authoritarian
   d. direct democracy

_____ **4.** Rulers attempt to control all aspects of citizens' lives in a
   a. dictatorship.
   b. monarchy.
   c. totalitarian government.
   d. democracy.

_____ **5.** People rule directly or elect representatives who act on their behalf in this system of government.
   a. dictatorship
   b. monarchy
   c. totalitarian government
   d. democracy

_____ **6.** Voters in a community meet to make laws and decisions for their community in a
   a. direct democracy.
   b. representative democracy.
   c. republic.
   d. monarchy.

_____ **7.** People elect representatives to make laws for them in a
   a. representative democracy.
   b. dictatorship.
   c. monarchy.
   d. direct democracy.

POST-READING QUICK CHECK After you have finished reading the section, list five of the services that government provides to its citizens.

1. _____

2. _____

3. _____

4. _____

5. _____

Guided Reading Strategies 2.2

Foundations of Government

READING THE SECTION As you read the section, fill in the missing information in the space provided.

1. Monarch of Britain when the colonies revolted _____

2. Colonial representatives who met in Philadelphia _____

3. Main author of the Declaration of Independence _____

4. U.S. document stating the protections government must provide_____

5. Basic rights to which all people are entitled _____

6. Loose association or league_____

7. Having independent power or autonomy _____

POST-READING QUICK CHECK After you have finished reading the section, pretend you are a delegate to the meeting held in 1787 to revise the Articles of Confederation. Write six suggestions you would take to the meeting.

1. _____

_____

2. _____

_____

3. _____

_____

4. _____

_____

5. _____

_____

6. _____

_____

CHAPTER  2   Guided Reading Strategies 2.3

Foundations of Government

READING THE SECTION As you read the section, match each of the terms in the left column with the correct definition from the right column in the space provided.

_____ **1.** delegates

_____ **2.** Parliament

_____ **3.** bicameral

_____ **4.** federalism

_____ **5.** unitary system

_____ **6.** compromise

_____ **7.** legislature

_____ **8.** ratification

_____ **9.** Federalists

_____ **10.** Antifederalists

a. sharing power between state and federal governments

b. government completely controlled by the national government

c. approval

d. great Britain's lawmaking body

e. representatives

f. agreement made when opposing sides yield to reach a solution

g. opposed ratification of the Constitution

h. legislature made up of two houses

i. lawmaking body

j. supporters of the Constitution

POST-READING QUICK CHECK After you have finished reading the section, fill in the missing information in the space provided.

1. _____ was elected president of the Constitutional Convention

2. _____ kept an accurate journal of convention proceedings

3. _____ was the oldest delegate at the Constitutional Convention

4. _____ became the temporary capital for the United States

5. _____ protected the rights of nobles against the British monarch in 1215

6. _____ included the right to petition and fair punishment for people found guilty of crimes in Great Britain

CHAPTER  **3**   Guided Reading Strategies 3.1

The U.S. Constitution

READING THE SECTION As you read the section, complete the following chart by listing the powers that the Constitution provides under each column heading.

Federal Government	State Governments	Shared Powers

POST-READING QUICK CHECK After you read the section, consider whether the statements below are true or false. In the space provided write a *T* beside true statements and an *F* beside false statements.

_____ **1.** The Preamble explains why the Declaration of Independence was written.

_____ **2.** The Mayflower Compact established consent of the governed for the Pilgrims.

_____ **3.** An amendment is a written change to the Constitution.

_____ **4.** The principle of majority rule in the United States disregards the rights of the minority.

_____ **5.** Limited government is government with defined restrictions on its power.

_____ **6.** Concurrent powers are powers left to the states.

_____ **7.** Rights guaranteed to the people of the United States are described in the Bill of Rights.

_____ **8.** State governments can raise funds through taxes, but the federal government cannot.

CHAPTER **3** — Guided Reading Strategies 3.2

The U.S. Constitution

READING THE SECTION As you read the section, fill in the missing information in the space provided.

1. Legislative branch

Main function (responsibility): **a.** _____

Two bodies: **b.** _____ and **c.** _____

A check it has over another branch of government: **d.** _____

2. Executive branch

Main function (responsibility): **e.** _____

Headed by (chief executive): **f.** _____

A check it has over another branch of government: **g.** _____

3. Judicial branch

Main function (responsibility): **h.** _____

Headed by: **i.** _____

A check it has over another branch of government: **j.** _____

POST-READING QUICK CHECK After you have finished reading the section, answer the following questions in the space provided.

1. Why was the system of checks and balances built into the Constitution?

_____

2. Which branch has the power to create lower federal courts? _____

3. What is the difference between the terms *separation of powers* and *federalism?*

_____

_____

4. How may Congress override a presidential veto? _____

5. Which branch controls the allocation of funds? _____

CHAPTER **3**   Guided Reading Strategies 3.3

The U.S. Constitution

READING THE SECTION As you read the section, fill in the blanks to complete the following sentences.

1. The U.S. Constitution can be called a "_____ document" because it can meet the changing conditions and needs of the country.

2. The Constitution can be adapted to meet changing needs in three ways:

_____, _____, and custom.

3. An _____ is a written change to the Constitution.

4. The section of the Constitution that outlines the process for changing the

Constitution is _____.

5. Formal approval by the states of a change to the Constitution is known as

_____.

6. If the people do not like the effects of an amendment, the amendment can be

_____.

7. _____ sometimes interprets the Constitution in new ways to

expand its authority to pass a certain law.

8. The _____ decides if new interpretations of the Constitution

are legal.

9. The president's _____, or group of advisers, is an example of a

change in the federal government that came about through custom and tradition.

10. Traditions of the federal government that are passed down through history are

sometimes called the _____ Constitution.

POST-READING QUICK CHECK After reading the section, answer the following question.

What are the two ways in which an amendment to the Constitution can be proposed? What are the two ways in which an amendment may be ratified?

CHAPTER 4   Guided Reading Strategies 4.1

Rights and Responsibilities

READING THE SECTION As you read the section, complete the following table by supplying the main rights protected by each amendment in the Bill of Rights.

Amendment	Main Rights
1. First	
2. Second	
3. Third	
4. Fourth	
5. Fifth	
6. Sixth	
7. Seventh	
8. Eighth	
9. Ninth	
10. Tenth	

POST-READING QUICK CHECK After you have finished reading the section, in the space provided, list three limits or exceptions to the rights listed in the Bill of Rights.

1. _____

_____

2. _____

_____

3. _____

_____

Name _____ Class _____ Date _____

Rights and Responsibilities

READING THE SECTION As you read the section, complete each sentence below by writing the appropriate term in the space provided.

1. The Twenty-fourth Amendment forbade the use of a(n) _____ as a voting qualification throughout the United States.

2. Direct election of senators by the people rather than through the state legislatures was established by the _____.

3. Women's _____ was granted by the Nineteenth Amendment.

4. The _____ freed slaves throughout the United States and its territories.

5. The Fourteenth Amendment was added to the Constitution after the _____ to protect the rights of African Americans.

6. The _____ lowered the voting age in the United States from 21 to 18.

7. Voting rights were granted to African Americans by the _____.

8. The _____ provides for due process and equal protection of the law for all Americans.

9. The Twenty-third Amendment gave people living in Washington, D.C., the right to vote for _____.

10. Rights guaranteed to all U.S. citizens are called _____.

POST-READING QUICK CHECK After you have finished reading the section, name four of the women who were instrumental in winning voting rights for U.S. women.

1. _____

2. _____

3. _____

4. _____

Name _____ Class _____ Date _____

READING THE SECTION As you read the section, complete each sentence by writing the correct letter in the space provided.

_____ **1.** Ignorance of the law
    a. is important.
    b. is a good excuse.
    c. is no excuse.
    d. aids in driving.

_____ **2.** Registration for the draft was reinstated in
    a. 1975.
    b. 1950.
    c. 1962.
    d. 1980.

_____ **3.** Citizens must, if called, report to serve as members of
    a. Congress.
    b. a jury.
    c. a local committee.
    d. a debate team.

_____ **4.** By voting, each citizen is
    a. deciding who will lead the country.
    b. going to be ignored.
    c. placing his or her name on a mailing list.
    d. wasting time.

_____ **5.** To cast their votes wisely, citizens should
    a. study law.
    b. be informed.
    c. watch TV.
    d. ask how their friends voted.

_____ **6.** Americans must tell government representatives their
    a. opinions on public issues.
    b. financial problems.
    c. hopes and dreams.
    d. travel plans.

_____ **7.** The quality of any government depends on the
    a. quality of people who serve.
    b. amount of taxes collected.
    c. quantity of political parties.
    d. president's political party.

_____ **8.** Cooperation with the police
    a. is not helpful.
    b. is an important way to help your community.
    c. will cause trouble.
    d. makes your neighbors angry.

POST-READING QUICK CHECK After you have finished reading the section, list the five responsibilities of citizenship in the spaces provided, and write an example for each.

1. _____

2. _____

3. _____

4. _____

5. _____

Name _____ Class _____ Date _____

READING THE SECTION As you read the section, answer the following questions in the spaces provided.

1. How many representatives are in the U.S. House of Representatives? _____

2. How many senators are in the U.S. Senate? _____

3. How is apportionment determined for the House of Representatives? How often does

this process occur? _____

_____

4. Explain how gerrymandering affects congressional district boundaries. _____

_____

5. List the three qualifications for holding the office of U.S. representative. _____

_____

6. List the three qualifications for holding the office of U.S. senator. _____

_____

7. How many years does a U.S. representative serve in one term? _____

8. How many years does a U.S. senator serve in one term? _____

9. What percentage of senators are up for re-election at one time? _____

POST-READING QUICK CHECK After you have finished reading the section, fill in the missing information in the space provided.

1. List three examples of the codes of conduct Congress has passed for its members.

   A._____

   B._____

   C._____

2. What is the difference between censure and the expulsion of a member of Congress?

_____

_____

Guided Reading Strategies 5.2

The Legislative Branch

READING THE SECTION As you read the section, match each of the following terms with the correct definitions in the space provided.

_____ 1. bills

_____ 2. caucuses

_____ 3. committees

_____ 4. conference committee

_____ 5. floor leader

_____ 6. joint committees

_____ 7. majority party

_____ 8. minority party

_____ 9. party whip

_____ 10. president *pro tempore*

_____ 11. select committees

_____ 12. seniority system

_____ 13. sessions

_____ 14. Speaker

_____ 15. standing committees

_____ 16. subcommittees

a. regular meetings of Congress

b. members of both houses of Congress meeting together

c. private meetings of congressional members by party

d. political party that controls the House or Senate

e. most powerful officer in the House of Representatives

f. assists floor leader in persuading members to support party

g. political party that has fewer members in the House or Senate

h. guides the party's proposed laws through Congress

i. presides over the Senate in vice president's absence

j. proposed laws

k. subdivisions (smaller groups) of Congress

l. committees made up of members from both houses

m. subdivisions of standing committees

n. permanent committees responsible for specific areas of business

o. handles issues not covered by standing committees

p. favors members with the most years of service

POST-READING QUICK CHECK After you have finished reading the section, answer the following questions in the space provided.

1. Who has the power to call a special session of Congress? _____

2. Who is customarily elected president *pro tempore*? _____

CHAPTER **5**

Guided Reading Strategies 5.3

The Legislative Branch

READING THE SECTION As you read the section, fill in the missing information in the spaces provided.

1. What is the elastic clause? _____

2. Name the federal officials that Congress may impeach (bring charges against).

_____

3. Which body of Congress has the power to impeach? _____

4. Where is the impeached official put on trial? _____

5. Under what circumstances would the vice president *not* preside over an

impeachment trial? _____

6. Who presides over the impeachment trial when the vice president does not?

_____

7. How many senators must vote for a conviction to remove an impeached official from

office? _____

8. Name the two presidents who have been impeached. _____

POST-READING QUICK CHECK After you have finished reading the section, fill in the information about Congress in the spaces provided.

1. Name the three special powers delegated to the House of Representatives. _____

_____

_____

_____

2. Name the four special powers delegated to the Senate. _____

_____

3. Write an example of how a member of Congress may serve a constituent.

_____

_____

CHAPTER  Guided Reading Strategies 5.4

The Legislative Branch

READING THE SECTION As you read the section, fill in the missing blanks with terms from the following list.

calendar	compromise bill	conference Committee	reported out
president	simple majority	standing committee	subcommittee
two-thirds	veto		

Bill is introduced in the House or Senate. ➔ Clerk numbers it HB# or SB# ➔ Bill is

referred to a Senate or House _____. ➔ Bill is sent to

_____ for review. ➔ Hearings are held on bill, recommendations

and changes are made. ➔ Committee votes and bill is _____ of

committee. ➔ Bill is placed on House or Senate _____. ➔ Bill is

debated on House or Senate floor. ➔ A(n) _____ is needed to pass

the bill in the House or Senate. ➔ The bill now goes to the other body of Congress, and

the process is repeated. ➔ If the bill passes in the other body of Congress, but the

versions are not identical, the bill goes to a _____ made up of

members from both houses. ➔ A revised bill or _____ then goes

back to both houses and must pass in both bodies with a simple majority. ➔ If the bill

passes in both houses, it then goes to the _____, who may sign it

into law. ➔ If instead the bill is rejected, then a _____ has taken

place. ➔ Congress may override a veto with a _____ majority of
both houses.

POST-READING QUICK CHECK After you have finished reading the section, answer the
questions in the space provided.

1. Name five people or groups that can propose laws to Congress. _____

_____

2. Bills concerning money must originate in the _____.

3. A debate on bills is generally limited to which body of Congress? _____

4. A(n)_____, or majority, must be present to do business.

5. Senators may try to keep a bill from coming up for a vote by making lengthy speeches
known as _____.

6. To limit debate, three fifths of the full Senate must vote for _____.

Name _____ Class _____ Date _____

READING THE SECTION As you read the section, answer the following questions in the spaces provided.

1. What are the three qualifications for the office of president of the United States?

_____

_____

_____

2. How many years does the president serve in one term? _____

3. Which amendment limited the president to two terms? _____

4. What is the annual salary for the president? _____

5. What are four benefits the president enjoys while in office? _____

_____

_____

_____

6. What job does the vice president officially have? _____

7. How many vice presidents have taken over the office of president? _____

POST-READING QUICK CHECK After reading the section, describe the changes the following laws or amendments made to the Constitution.

1. Presidential Succession (1947) _____

_____

_____

_____

2. The Twenty-fifth Amendment (1967) _____

_____

_____

_____

The Executive Branch

READING THE SECTION As you read the section, write in the duties the president performs in the following different roles.

1. Chief executive

    1. _____

    2. _____

    3. _____

    4. _____

2. Commander in chief

    1. _____

    2. _____

3. Chief diplomat or foreign policy leader

    1. _____

    2. _____

    3. _____

4. Judicial powers

    1. _____

    2. _____

5. Other presidential roles

    1. _____

    2. _____

    3. _____

POST-READING QUICK CHECK After reading the section, describe the following law in the space provided.

War Powers Act (1973) _____

_____

_____

_____

CHAPTER **6** Guided Reading Strategies 6.3

The Executive Branch

READING THE SECTION As you read the section, decide whether the following statements are true or false. Write a *T* in front of the true statements and an *F* in front of the false statements in the space provided.

_____ **1.** The National Security Council advises in matters concerning the environment and water safety.

_____ **2.** The secretary of state assists and advises the president in foreign affairs and foreign policy.

_____ **3.** The head of the Department of Justice is the secretary of justice.

_____ **4.** Visas allow U.S. citizens to travel to foreign countries.

_____ **5.** Consuls represent the United States concerning trade and commerce in foreign countries.

_____ **6.** The Joint Chiefs of Staff include the highest ranking officers of the army, navy, and air force.

_____ **7.** The National Park Service and the U.S. Fish and Wildlife Service are two divisions within the Department of the Interior.

_____ **8.** The National School Lunch Program and Food Stamps are managed by divisions within the Department of Agriculture.

_____ **9.** The Census Bureau, which counts U.S. population every decade, is part of the Department of Labor.

_____ **10.** Education loans to veterans are administered through the Department of Education.

POST-READING QUICK CHECK After reading the section, write the word or words that would make the false statements above true. Write the number of the false statement with the correction(s).

_____

_____

_____

_____

_____

CHAPTER 6   Guided Reading Strategies 6.4

The Executive Branch

READING THE SECTION As you read the section, write the job or duty of each of the following independent agencies or regulatory commissions in the space provided.

1. U.S. Commission on Civil Rights _____

2. Farm Credit Administration _____

3. Small Business Administration _____

4. National Aeronautics and Space Administration _____

5. Office of Personnel Management _____

6. General Services Administration _____

7. Federal Election Commission _____

8. Consumer Product Safety Commission _____

9. Securities and Exchange Commission _____

10. National Labor Relations Board _____

POST-READING QUICK CHECK After reading the section, fill in the blanks with the correct answers to complete each statement.

1. The _____ appoints the heads of the regulatory commissions.

2. Appointments to the regulatory commissions must be approved by the

_____ .

3. About three million people work in the federal _____, which performs the day-to-day work of the executive branch.

4. The more than 65 independent agencies that _____ created assist the president in carrying out his duties.

5. Independent agencies that bring violators to court are called

_____ .

Name _____ Class _____ Date _____

CHAPTER 7   Guided Reading Strategies 7.1

The Judicial Branch

READING THE SECTION As you read the section, match each of the following terms with the correct definition in the space provided.

_____ **1.** administrative law   **a.** laws passed by lawmaking bodies

_____ **2.** appeal   **b.** laws created by government agencies

_____ **3.** common law   **c.** an earlier decision and example for others to follow

_____ **4.** constitutional law   **d.** a trial jury of 6 to 12 people

_____ **5.** cross-examination   **e.** law that comes from judges' decisions

_____ **6.** hung jury   **f.** men and women of a trial jury

_____ **7.** jurors   **g.** law based on the Constitution

_____ **8.** jury duty   **h.** jury decision in a court case

_____ **9.** petit jury   **i.** evidence given by a witness in a court case

_____ **10.** precedent   **j.** jury that cannot reach a verdict

_____ **11.** statutory laws   **k.** selection to serve on a panel of jurors

_____ **12.** testimony   **l.** higher court review of a case

_____ **13.** verdict   **m.** defense attorney's right to question a witness

POST-READING QUICK CHECK After reading the section, write the correct answers in the spaces provided.

List the rights a person accused of a crime has under the U.S. Constitution.

1. _____

2. _____

3. _____

4. _____

CHAPTER **7**  Guided Reading Strategies 7.2

The Judicial Branch

READING THE SECTION After reading the section, fill in the blanks with the correct answer to complete each statement.

1. District courts would normally have original _____ in cases.

2. Courts of appeal have _____ jurisdiction and are also known

as _____ courts.

3. U.S. marshals deliver _____, which are court orders that require a person to appear in court.

4. District court officials who decide if a case should go before a grand jury are called

_____.

5. In a struggle with the Internal Revenue Service, a disgruntled tax payer could appeal

to the _____.

6. Federal judges serve for _____. They may be

_____ or removed from office for serious misconduct.

7. Federal judges are appointed by the _____ and must be

confirmed by the _____.

8. Puerto Rico and Guam each have _____ to administer justice to the people of those U.S. possessions.

POST-READING QUICK CHECK After reading the section, write the appropriate answer(s) in the space provided.

1. Name the nine types of cases that can be brought before a federal court.

_____

_____

_____

2. What is the job or function of the courts of appeal? _____

3. Name the three types of cases that go before the Supreme Court. _____

_____

CHAPTER **7**

Guided Reading Strategies 7.3

The Judicial Branch

READING THE SECTION As you read the section, complete each sentence by writing the correct letter in the space provided.

_____ **1.** The return of a case to a lower court for a new trial is called a
   a. remand.
   b. docket.
   c. brief.

_____ **2.** The main argument made by a lawyer in a case is called a
   a. remand.
   b. docket.
   c. brief.

_____ **3.** When a justice agrees with the majority decision but for differing reasons, he or she might write a(n)
   a. opinion.
   b. concurring opinion.
   c. dissenting opinion.

_____ **4.** The justice who disagrees with the majority might write a(n)
   a. opinion to serve.
   b. concurring opinion.
   c. dissenting opinion.

_____ **5.** The case that established the "reading of rights" to a suspect was
   a. *Miranda* v. *Arizona.*
   b. *Brown* v. *Board of Education.*
   c. *Plessy* v. *Ferguson.*

_____ **6.** The case that established the "separate but equal rights" was
   a. *Miranda* v. *Arizona.*
   b. *Brown* v. *Board of Education.*
   c. *Plessy* v. *Ferguson.*

POST-READING QUICK CHECK After you have finished reading the section, write the answers in the spaces provided.

1. What can Congress do if the Supreme Court declares a law unconstitutional?

_____

_____

_____

2. How did President Franklin D. Roosevelt try to change the nature of the Supreme Court? Why do you think he wanted to make this change in the Court?

_____

_____

Guided Reading Strategies 8.1

State Government

READING THE SECTION As you read the section, list the information in the spaces provided for the reserved and concurrent powers.

State powers (reserved)

1. _____

2. _____

3. _____

4. _____

5. _____

6. _____

7. _____

Shared powers (concurrent)

8. _____

9. _____

10. _____

11. _____

POST-READING QUICK CHECK After reading the section, fill in the blanks with the correct answers to complete each statement.

1. The _____ protects the rights of state governments.

2. In 1787 the _____ stated the stipulations for territories to become states.

3. In the _____, states agree to accept decisions of courts in other states.

4. Returning fugitives to other states is known as _____.

5. Some of the items that most state constitutions contain are _____ _____ _____.

CHAPTER **8**   Guided Reading Strategies 8.2

State Government

READING THE SECTION As you read the section, match each of the following terms with the correct definition in the space provided.

_____ **1.** initiative

a. one-house legislature

_____ **2.** item veto

b. rejection of one portion of an appropriation bill

_____ **3.** propostition

c. starting a petition for a new bill or law

_____ **4.** recall

d. proposed law put on the ballot

_____ **5.** referendum

e. voter approval of legislative bills

_____ **6.** unicameral

f. an election held to remove an elected official from office

POST-READING QUICK CHECK After reading the section, answer the following questions in the spaces provided.

1. What court case in 1964 established that all state election districts be equal?

_____

2. Which state has the only unicameral legislature? _____

3. Which state has the smallest legislature, with only 40 representatives and 20 senators?

_____

4. Which state only pays state legislators $10,000 annually? _____

5. Which state pays state legislators $79,500 annually? _____

6. What state legislature meets the entire period for a two-year session? _____

7. If a bill passes in both houses but not in identical forms, what would be the next step

in the lawmaking process? _____

CHAPTER  8

Guided Reading Strategies 8.3

State Government

READING THE SECTION As you read the section, write an example for each of the following duties that governors perform.

chief legislator   **1.** _____

chief executive   **2.** _____

political party leader   **3.** _____

other   **4.** _____

POST-READING QUICK CHECK After reading the section, fill in the blanks with the appropriate answer concerning the executive branch.

1. If the governor dies or is removed from office, the _____ would be next in line to become governor.

2. The executive official in charge of keeping state records and carrying out election laws is the _____.

3. The _____ handles state legal matters.

4. Handling state funds is the job of the _____.

5. The _____ examines state financial records and payments.

6. Carrying out policies of the state board of education is performed by the

_____, who also handles the distribution of state funds to local districts.

7. The orders that set up methods of enforcing laws are known as

_____.

8. Jobs given to people as a reward, or thanks for their work for a political party during

the campaign are known as _____.

9. The written order signed by the state auditor to pay a bill is called a(n)

_____.

 **CHAPTER 8** Guided Reading Strategies 8.4

State Government

READING THE SECTION As you read the section, match each of the following terms with the correct definitions in the space provided.

_____ **1.** civil cases

_____ **2.** complaint

_____ **3.** criminal cases

_____ **4.** general trial courts

_____ **5.** justice of the peace

_____ **6.** municipal courts

_____ **7.** penal code

_____ **8.** plaintiff

_____ **9.** small claims court

a. set of criminal laws

b. deal with violations of the law

c. person filing the lawsuit

d. another name for a lawsuit

e. deal with disputes between individuals and businesses

f. courts in larger cities that are divided to hear specific cases

g. courts that hear civil cases involving small sums of money

h. elected official who presides over minor cases in justice court

i. handle major criminal and civil cases

POST-READING QUICK CHECK After reading the section, write the correct answers in the spaces provided.

1. How do courts of appeals cases differ from general trial court cases?

_____

_____

_____

Name the two ways state supreme court judges are selected.

2. _____

3. _____

CHAPTER 9   Guided Reading Strategies 9.1
Local Government

READING THE SECTION As you read the section, name the term or office that each of the following statements describes.

1. Basic plan for local government that defines its powers, responsibilities, and organization _____

2. Local government incorporated by the state _____

3. Regulations that govern the community _____

4. The parts most states are divided into _____

5. Head law enforcement official for counties _____

6. The county government, courthouse, and county jail are located here _____

7. Person who records births, deaths, marriages, and election results _____

8. Handles county funds and collects taxes if there is no tax collector _____

9. Examines the financial records for the county _____

10. Represents the state government in county trials and is sometimes called the prosecutor _____

11. Some county governments have been reorganized to create this position to ensure efficiency _____

POST-READING QUICK CHECK After you have finished reading the section, list the answers in the spaces provided.

1. List six services that local governments provide for citizens. _____

_____

_____

2. How do local governments become municipalities? Why would this be beneficial?

_____

_____

CHAPTER  Guided Reading Strategies 9.2

Local Government

READING THE SECTION As you read the section, match each of the following terms with the correct definitions in the space provided.

_____ **1.** Voters elect officials to attend town meetings and make decisions for them in this type of local government

_____ **2.** Law enforcement official for a township

_____ **3.** Form of local government that started in the New England colonies and included outlying farms

_____ **4.** Units of government created in the Northwest Territory that sometimes occupied the same area as a congressional township

_____ **5.** Public meeting where residents can discuss and vote on issues

_____ **6.** Charter from the state that addresses a special need for a specific area

_____ **7.** Small units of local government, divided out of counties, that started in the Middle Atlantic states

_____ **8.** Form of local government that started in the New England colonies and included the homes of the settlers and other buildings

_____ **9.** The executive of the small council in a village or borough who is elected by voters

a. town

b. village

c. constable

d. town meeting

e. representative town meeting

f. special district

g. townships

h. civil townships

i. mayor

POST-READING QUICK CHECK After you have finished reading the section, answer the following questions in the spaces provided.

1. How can residents organize their local community into a village or borough form of

government? _____

_____

_____

2. What is the governing body of local school districts called? How are the officials that

make up that body selected? _____

_____

CHAPTER **9**   Guided Reading Strategies 9.3

Local Government

READING THE SECTION As you read the section, fill in the missing information to complete the following chart.

Three Forms of City Government	Main Points of Each Form
mayor-council	1. 2. 3.
commission	1. 2. 3.
council-manager	1. 2. 3.

POST-READING QUICK CHECK After you have finished reading the section, list the answers to the following questions in the spaces provided.

1. How does a city establish home rule? What powers does it give city government?

_____

2. Which of the three types of city government is the oldest and most commonly used?

_____

3. Where was the commission form of city government introduced?

_____

4. Where was the council-manager form of government first set up?

_____

5. Which of the three forms of city government is run most like a business and could (at least in theory) bypass partisan politics?

_____

CHAPTER **9**   Guided Reading Strategies 9.4

Local Government

READING THE SECTION As you read the section, find the information needed to answer each of the following questions, and write the answers in the spaces provided.

1. What are grants-in-aid? Give one example in your area or state.

_____

_____

2. What are block grants? Give one example in your area or state.

_____

_____

3. Write five examples of how federal funding and the accompanying regulations provide uniformity and consistency throughout the United States.

  a. _____

  b. _____

  c. _____

  d. _____

  e. _____

POST-READING QUICK CHECK After reading the section, find the following information concerning your school district.

Federal guidelines and regulations must be followed for state and local governments to be eligible for federal funds. Look into a program in your local government or school district that receives federal funds and briefly describe the guidelines for receiving those funds.

_____

_____

_____

_____

 Guided Reading Strategies 10.1

Electing Leaders

READING THE SECTION Read the following statements and write a *T* in front of the true statements and an *F* in front of the false statements. If false, explain why.

_____ **1.** Political parties are made up of citizens with similar views on public issues.

_____

_____ **2.** President George Washington encouraged the two-party system and thought it

was healthy for the country. _____

_____ **3.** Alexander Hamilton's ideas and followers formed the Democratic-Republican

Party. _____

_____ **4.** Political parties nominate the individuals who run for election to public office.

_____

_____ **5.** The Republican Party was formed in 1854 and opposed the spread of slavery

into the new territories. _____

_____ **6.** The Democratic Party of today stems from Andrew Jackson's desire to

represent the common people. _____

_____ **7.** The multiparty systems found in many European countries have the

advantage of easily forming stable governments. _____

_____ **8.** One-party systems are examples of dictatorships and totalitarian governments.

_____

_____ **9.** In 1912 Theodore Roosevelt formed the Populist party. _____

_____**10.** Third-party views and platforms often are adopted by mainstream parties.

_____

POST-READING QUICK CHECK After you have finished reading the section, write the advantages of the two-party system over one-party or multiparty systems.

_____

_____

CHAPTER **10** Guided Reading Strategies 10.2

Electing Leaders

READING THE SECTION As you read the section, fill in the correct information about the different types of committees in the spaces provided on the chart.

COMMITTEES	METHODS OF MEMBER AND CHAIRPERSON SELECTION	DUTIES AND RESPONSIBILITIES
Local Committees		
State Committees		
National Committees		

POST-READING QUICK CHECK After you have finished reading the section, answer the following questions concerning political parties and campaigns.

1. How did the Federal Election Campaign Act reform campaign contributions? What

agency monitors contributions? _____

_____

_____

_____

2. What are the eligibility requirements for candidates to obtain matching public funds

in federal elections? _____

_____

_____

_____

_____

CHAPTER  **10**   Guided Reading Strategies 10.3

Electing Leaders

READING THE SECTION As you read the section, match the following terms with the appropriate definition by writing the correct letter in the space provided.

_____ **1.** closed primary

_____ **2.** general election

_____ **3.** grassroots

_____ **4.** independent voters

_____ **5.** open primary

_____ **6.** primary election

_____ **7.** runoff

_____ **8.** secret ballot

_____ **9.** split ticket

_____ **10.** straight ticket

a. first election to choose party candidates to run in a later election

b. election in which voters may vote for candidates of either party

c. ballots marked in privacy

d. voting for all candidates from one political party

e. voting for candidates from more than one political party

f. election in which voters choose their leaders

g. election held when neither of the two leading candidates in an election receive a majority of the votes

h. voters who are not members of a political party

i. support from individuals at the local level rather than from political parties

j. election in which only registered party members can vote to choose the party's candidates

POST-READING QUICK CHECK After you have finished reading the section, write the answers to the questions in the spaces provided.

1. What would disqualify a voter in most states? _____

_____

2. How are independent candidates placed on the general ballot in an election?

_____

_____

 **CHAPTER 10** Guided Reading Strategies 10.4

Electing Leaders

READING THE SECTION As you read the section, answer the following questions concerning the election process in the spaces provided.

1. What are the three ways that states determine which state delegates attend the national party convention?

   a. _____

   b. _____

   c. _____

2. What are the three ways of delegate voting at the national convention (for the states that hold presidential primaries)?

   a. _____

   b. _____

   c. _____

3. What decisions are made at the national party conventions?

   a. _____

   b. _____

POST-READING QUICK CHECK After you have finished reading the section, answer the following question on the electoral process in the space provided.

Explain how the electoral college works in electing the President of the United States and what role the popular vote plays in the process.

_____

_____

_____

CHAPTER **11**   Guided Reading Strategies 11.1
The Political System

READING THE SECTION As you read the section, complete each sentence below by writing the appropriate term in the space provided.

1. The total of the opinions held concerning a particular issue is called

_____.

2. Various forms of communication, or the _____, includes television, radio, newspapers, books, films, and magazines.

3. The stating of information to persuade or influence is called_____.

4. When information is used to fool people, but presented in a factual manner, it is

called _____.

5. Advertising would be an example of _____, because people are aware that the intention is to influence them.

6. Endorsements from famous individuals such as professional athletes are considered

_____, one type of propaganda technique.

7. Jumping on the _____ is a type of propaganda in which peer pressure techniques are used to get people to join the crowd.

8. The use of negative or unpleasant descriptions or labels is often used in campaigns

and is known as the _____ propaganda technique.

9. Using facts or statistics in a manner that favors a particular product, idea, or candi-

date is called _____.

10. _____ are used to measure public opinion and choose a representative sample of the population to question.

POST-READING QUICK CHECK After you have finished reading this section, describe the correct way to administer or conduct a public opinion poll.

_____

_____

_____

CHAPTER **11** Guided Reading Strategies 11.2
The Political System

READING THE SECTION As you read the section, fill in the blanks with the correct information in the space provided.

1. Organizations of people with a common interest that try to influence government policies

   _____

2. Another name for an interest or pressure group

   _____

3. A person who is paid by an interest group to represent and work with policymakers

   _____

4. List the three types of interest groups.

   _____

   _____

   _____

5. List three different common interest groups found in the United States.

   _____

   _____

   _____

POST-READING QUICK CHECK After you have finished reading the section, answer the following questions in the spaces provided.

1. What are some of the methods that lobbyists use to help lawmakers?

   _____

   _____

2. Describe how the Lobbying Disclosure Act of 1995 helps the government keep track of interest groups and their financial influence.

   _____

   _____

CHAPTER **11**

Guided Reading Strategies 11.3

The Political System

READING THE SECTION As you read the section, write the correct information or examples concerning government participation in the spaces provided.

1. List five reasons why the voter turnout rate is lower in the United States than in most other democratic nations.

a. _____

b. _____

c. _____

d. _____

e. _____

2. List five ways that individuals may participate in the campaign process in their community.

a. _____

b. _____

c. _____

d. _____

e. _____

POST-READING QUICK CHECK After reading the section, answer the following questions in the spaces provided.

1. How do political action committees (PACs) work and allow groups to contribute to individual candidates in an election?

_____

_____

2. How can individuals voice opinions and concerns to local officials and congress-members?

_____

_____

CHAPTER  12   Guided Reading Strategies 12.1

Paying for Government

READING THE SECTION As you read the section, decide which of the following statements are true and which are false. Write a *T* in front of the true statements and write a *F* in front of the false statements in the spaces provided. If false, explain why.

_____ **1.** One of the largest expenditures of the federal government is national defense.

_____

_____ **2.** The main source of government revenue is the national debt.

_____

_____ **3.** Under the taxation principle concerning ability to pay, there are different

rates for different age groups. _____

_____ **4.** Equal application of taxes would make sales taxes the same rate for similar

items. _____

_____ **5.** Scheduled payments of taxes would include withholdings from workers'

paychecks. _____

_____ **6.** Fees are sources of revenue from people who break certain laws, such as those

regarding traffic. _____

_____ **7.** The fees charged for drivers licenses and automobile licenses are a major

source of revenue for state governments. _____

_____ **8.** Government borrowing from individuals would be an example of a fine.

_____

_____ **9.** Bonds include a promise to repay the amount borrowed, with interest, on the

maturity date. _____

POST-READING QUICK CHECK After you have finished reading the section, think about the types of taxes that citizens pay in the United States. List some other fair ways that federal, state, or local governments could raise funds.

_____

_____

CHAPTER **12**   Guided Reading Strategies 12.2

Paying for Government

READING THE SECTION As you read the section, match each of the following terms with the correct definition and write the letter in front of the matching term in the space provided.

_____ **1.** deductions

_____ **2.** estate tax

_____ **3.** excise tax

_____ **4.** exemptions

_____ **5.** gift tax

_____ **6.** income taxes

_____ **7.** inheritance tax

_____ **8.** personal property

_____ **9.** profit

_____ **10.** progressive tax

_____ **11.** property tax

_____ **12.** real estate

_____ **13.** regressive tax

_____ **14.** sales tax

_____ **15.** Social Security

_____ **16.** tariff

_____ **17.** taxable income

a. deductions for self and dependent

b. high-income groups are taxed at a larger percentage than low-income groups

c. income a business has left after paying its expenses

d. tax on workers that provides income to the disabled and retirees

e. consists of land, buildings, and other structures

f. tax on imported goods

g. tax collected on products sold

h. expenses like charitable contributions and mortgage interest

i. tax based on the portion of an estate received by an individual

j. tax on luxury and nonessential items

k. federal tax on the wealth a person leaves after death

l. amount on which tax is paid after all subtractions

m. tax on a gift worth more than $10,000

n. includes stocks, bonds, cars, boats, jewelry

o. taxes on the earnings of individuals and companies

p. chief source of income for most local governments

q. tax that takes a larger percentage of income from low-income groups than from high-income groups

POST-READING QUICK CHECK After you have finished reading the section, decide which taxes seem the most fair. Which taxes do you think are most unfair? Explain your answer.

_____

_____

CHAPTER **12**   Guided Reading Strategies 12.3

Paying for Government

READING THE SECTION Read through the following descriptions. As you read the section provide the correct term for each description in the space provided.

1. _____ Agency of the Treasury Department that handles the federal collection of taxes

2. _____ Federal agency in charge of collecting tariffs on imported goods

3. _____ State or local official responsible for ensuring public funds are spent as authorized

4. _____ Federal official(s) responsible for planning the federal budget

5. _____ Federal body that must turn the federal budget into law

6. _____ Federal agency that evaluates the effectiveness and efficiency of executive agencies

7. _____ When government revenue equals government expenditures

8. _____ When government collects more than it spends

9. _____ When government spends more than it collects

10. _____ An accountant's examination of every item of income and expenditure

POST-READING QUICK CHECK After you have read the section, explain in the space provided how the legislative branch finalizes the federal budget and authorizes the spending of funds.

_____

_____

_____

Name _____ Class _____ Date _____

Citizenship and the Family

READING THE SECTION As you read the section, complete each sentence by writing the correct letter in the space provided.

_____ **1.** The percentage of Americans who live in rural areas today is
  a. 50 percent.
  b. 25 percent.
  c. 10 percent.
  d. 20 percent.

_____ **2.** Many Americans moved to urban areas because of
  a. new inventions.
  b. the rise of factories.
  c. farm machinery improvements.
  d. all of the above

_____ **3.** _____ percent of American families with children under 18 live in single-parent families.
  a. 27
  b. 25
  c. 50
  d. 62

_____ **4.** The average age for women to marry in 1998 was
  a. 20.3.
  b. 22.8.
  c. 25.0.
  d. 26.7.

_____ **5.** Which of the following is not a reason for delayed marriages?
  a. economic necessity
  b. growing acceptance of singlehood
  c. finishing education and starting a career
  d. living together

_____ **6.** Almost _____ of single-parent families headed by females live in poverty.
  a. 20 percent
  b. 30 percent
  c. 40 percent
  d. 50 percent

POST-READING QUICK CHECK After you have finished reading the section, list some of the reasons why there are so many blended families in U.S. society today. Name some of the added stresses placed on these families.

_____

_____

_____

_____

_____

_____

_____

Guided Reading Strategies 13.2

Citizenship and the Family

READING THE SECTION As you read the section, fill in the blanks with the correct term in the space provided.

1. Laws that govern family life, including marriage and divorce, are passed by the

_____.

2. In most states, people under the age of 18 are required by law to have

_____ before they can marry.

3. Waiting periods and a(n) _____ are required in some states before a couple can obtain a marriage license.

4. Doctors and teachers must report suspected cases of _____ to the proper authorities.

5. Children who have been abused may be placed in _____ to be cared for properly.

6. A person who is appointed by the state court to care for a minor would be the

minor's _____.

7. To _____ a child is to legally establish him or her as a member of a family.

8. In a(n) _____, couples do not have to charge their partners with grounds, just irreconcilable differences.

9. Division of property, _____ of children, and child support are some of the issues and decisions that divorcing couples must face.

10. According to social scientists, one reason for the high divorce rate in the United States

is the _____ of women who work outside the home.

POST-READING QUICK CHECK After you have finished reading the section, list some possible solutions or ways to keep more marriages together and help bring the divorce rate down in the United States.

_____

_____

_____

CHAPTER 13   Guided Reading Strategies 13.3

Citizenship and the Family

READING THE SECTION As you read the section, complete the following chart by filling in the correct information concerning families and their chief functions in American society.

Five Functions Of Families	Description/Example of Each Function
1.	A.
2.	B.
3.	C.
4.	D.
5.	E.

POST-READING QUICK CHECK After you have finished reading the section, list some ways in the space provided that you could be more (1) respectful of, (2) helpful to, and (3) considerate of family members.

1. _____

   _____

2. _____

   _____

3. _____

   _____

CHAPTER 14 Guided Reading Strategies 14.1

Citizenship in School

READING THE SECTION As you read the section, complete the following statements by filling in the blanks.

1. The two main reasons that Americans place a high value on education are the

   development of _____ and the _____.

2. The first state to pass a law setting up public schools was _____ in 1647.

3. In the early 1800s, _____ worked to establish a public school system.

4. Children three and four years old may attend _____ to learn how to play and get along with other children.

5. High schools that provide a college preparatory curriculum are known as

   _____ high schools.

6. Technical and _____ high schools provide occupational training.

7. High schools that design their curriculum to attract certain types of students are

   called _____.

8. Two-year _____ are often supported by tax money and provide specialized job training and prep courses for transferring to a four-year college.

9. Students with special needs are often taught in regular classrooms when possible, a

   practice known as _____.

10. Enrichment instruction is often provided for _____ students.

POST-READING QUICK CHECK After you have finished reading the section, answer the following questions in the spaces provided.

1. What are the five traditional values found in the American educational process?

   _____

2. What are some of the challenges facing the American public school system? What are some possible solutions to these problems?

   _____

Guided Reading Strategies 14.2

Citizenship in School

READING THE SECTION As you read the section, write each of the seven goals of schools in the space beside the correct definition.

1. Teaching basics—reading, math, etc. _____

_____

2. Teaching socialization skills _____

_____

3. Teaching good hygiene, fitness, etc. _____

_____

4. Career education, preparing for future _____

_____

5. Teaching democratic principles _____

_____

6. Teaching respectful attitudes _____

_____

7. Teaching hobbies and enrichment _____

_____

POST-READING QUICK CHECK After you have finished reading the section, fill in the information asked for in the spaces provided.

1. Write the list of study habits and textbook hints that can help you become a better organized student.

_____

_____

2. List the values and skills that extracurricular activities can provide to help students later in life.

_____

_____

CHAPTER  **14**   Guided Reading Strategies 14.3

Citizenship in School

READING THE SECTION As you read the section, match each of the following terms with the correct definition by placing the correct letter in the space provided.

_____ **1.** conditioning

_____ **2.** creativity

_____ **3.** critical thinking

_____ **4.** experience

_____ **5.** habit

_____ **6.** insight

_____ **7.** motivation

_____ **8.** prejudice

a. an action that is performed automatically without thinking

b. direct observation of or participation in events

c. using and applying one's own knowledge to come up with a solution

d. opinion that is not based on careful and reasonable investigation of the facts

e. behavior or action exhibited with expectations of reward or satisfaction

f. ability to find new ways of thinking and doing things

g. type of reasoning that involves a number of steps to reach decisions and solve problems

h. internal drive that stirs people and directs their behavior and attitudes

POST-READING QUICK CHECK After you have finished reading the section, think of a current problem at home or school and then use the critical-thinking steps to come up with a possible solution. List each step before writing the applicable information for your particular problem.

_____

_____

_____

_____

_____

_____

_____

_____

_____

_____

_____

_____

_____

CHAPTER **15** Guided Reading Strategies 15.1

Citizenship in the Community

READING THE SECTION As you read the section, complete the following sentences by filling in the blanks.

1. The largest American cities were the Atlantic port cities of Boston, New York, and

   Philadelphia in the North and _____ in the South.

2. _____ was an important port city at the mouth of the Mississippi River.

3. Two inland city ports, _____ and _____ are easy-to-reach stopping points on the upper Mississippi River.

4. _____ owes much of its growth to iron-ore deposits located nearby in the Mesabi Range.

5. Because early textile mills needed waterpower, many _____ communities were settled near waterfalls.

6. Mixed farms—where pigs, cows, and chickens are raised and a variety of crops are

   grown—can be found in _____.

7. In _____, you will find a large number of dairy farms.

8. Cattle ranches, tobacco, and cotton farms can be found in _____.

9. Sugarcane and pineapple plantations will be found in _____.

10. _____ are communities located on the outskirts of a city.

11. Cities with populations of 2,500 or more are considered _____.

12. There are about 200 _____ in the United States today. They consist of a large city and the surrounding towns and suburbs.

13. The giant urban area that includes the metropolitan areas of Boston, New York City,

    Philadelphia, Baltimore, and Washington, D.C., form a(n) _____ along the Atlantic coast.

POST-READING QUICK CHECK After you have finished reading the section, think of some other U.S. cities (other than those mentioned in the section) that are located at crossroads. List five cities and the transportation routes that they are near.

_____

_____

Name _____ Class _____ Date _____

Citizenship in the Community

READING THE SECTION As you read the section, fill in the blanks in the following outline on the reasons people live in communities.

1. Communication: Passing along of information, ideas, and beliefs from one person to another. List eight types of communication.

a. _____   d. _____   g. _____

b. _____   e. _____   h. _____

c. _____   f. _____

2. Recreation: Relaxation or amusement by playing or doing something different from one's usual activities. List eight types of recreation.

a. _____   d. _____   g. _____

b. _____   e. _____   h. _____

c. _____   f. _____

3. Community services: Provide better services to meet certain citizen needs. List six types of community services.

a. _____   c. _____   e. _____

b. _____   d. _____   f. _____

4. Local government: Provides laws and regulations needed to keep order. List three groups that maintain peace and order.

a. _____   b. _____   c. _____

POST-READING QUICK CHECK After reading the section, list four purposes that good community recreational facilities serve.

1. _____

2. _____

3. _____

4. _____

CHAPTER **15**   Guided Reading Strategies 15.3

Citizenship in the Community

READING THE SECTION As you read the section, write the correct term to fill in the blanks and complete each statement.

1. Some citizenship services are required by law, which means they are

_____.

2. Two examples of compulsory laws are _____ and

_____.

3. In 1999, a Las Vegas, New Mexico, advisory board set up a program called

_____, to create better communication between youth and city leaders.

4. To clear slums and reduce congestion, the citizens of _____ cleared and rebuilt a large part of their business district.

5. A successful program to better schools, playgrounds, and museums was implemented

in _____.

6. A campaign to clean up the pollution that steel mills and factories emitted was

successful in _____.

7. Volunteers collect money for _____ and to help the sick, elderly, and disabled.

8. Examples of a(n) _____ would be student-parent-teacher organizations, volunteer firefighters, and hospital volunteers.

9. A large national volunteer group, the _____, has more than one million volunteers.

POST-READING QUICK CHECK After reading the section, write down examples of how you can be a good global citizen.

_____

_____

_____

_____

_____

CHAPTER  **16**   Guided Reading Strategies 16.1

Citizenship and the Law

READING THE SECTION As you read the section, match each of the following terms with the correct definition in the space provided.

_____ **1.** aggravated assault

_____ **2.** arson

_____ **3.** burglary

_____ **4.** crime

_____ **5.** criminal

_____ **6.** embezzlement

_____ **7.** felonies

_____ **8.** forcible rape

_____ **9.** fraud

_____ **10.** grand larceny

_____ **11.** homicide

_____ **12.** larceny

_____ **13.** misdemeanors

_____ **14.** petty larceny

_____ **15.** robbery

_____ **16.** vandalism

_____ **17.** victimless crime

_____ **18.** white-collar crime

a. killing of one person by another person

b. act that breaks the law

c. physical injury done intentionally to another

d. serious crimes like homicide

e. forcible and illegal entry with intention to steal

f. the willful destruction of property

g. destruction of property by setting fire to it

h. crime committed for illegal gain at the workplace

i. less-serious offenses like traffic violations

j. taking money entrusted to one's care for one's own use

k. theft of property without use of force or violence

l. taking someone else's money or property dishonestly

m. theft of goods of more than a certain amount

n. crime that involves both property and persons

o. person who commits any type of crime

p. when a criminal does not violate another person's rights

q. theft of goods under a certain amount

r. sexual violation of a person by force

POST-READING QUICK CHECK After you read the section, list three reasons why the crime rate is so high in the United States. Also list three ways to prevent crime.

_____

_____

_____

CHAPTER **16**

Guided Reading Strategies 16.2

Citizenship and the Law

READING THE SECTION As you read the section, complete each sentence by writing the letter of the correct term in the space provided.

_____ **1.** The police, courts, and corrections facilities are known as
   a. capital punishment.
   b. rehabilitation.
   c. the criminal justice system.
   d. community policing.

_____ **2.** The authorization from the court needed by police when there is no witness linking the suspect to the crime is known as a(n)
   a. arrest warrant.
   b. probable cause.
   c. arraignment
   d. plea bargain.

_____ **3.** A plea of guilty or not guilty from the accused occurs during the
   a. arraignment.
   b. indictment.
   c. corrections.
   d. plea bargain.

_____ **4.** During a trial, the government's side of the case is presented by the
   a. defense.
   b. corrections.
   c. defendant.
   d. prosecution.

_____ **5.** A reasonable amount of doubt as to a defendant's guilt will cause the jury to vote
   a. to arraign.
   b. to indict.
   c. to acquit.
   d. to parole.

_____ **6.** Many cases never go to trial because the accused pleads guilty to a lesser charge, which is called a
   a. sentence.
   b. plea bargain.
   c. parole.
   d. rehabilitation.

_____ **7.** Imprisonment, parole, and capital punishment are part of the system of
   a. corrections.
   b. prosecution.
   c. rehabilitation.
   d. deterrence.

_____ **8.** The early release of prisoners who show signs of rehabilitation is called
   a. deterrence.
   b. prosecution.
   c. corrections.
   d. parole.

POST-READING QUICK CHECK After you have finished reading the section, list the pros and cons of capital punishment. Use the U.S. Constitution as the basis for your arguments.

_____

_____

_____

CHAPTER **16**   Guided Reading Strategies 16.3

Citizenship and the Law

READING THE SECTION As you read the section, place a "T" in front of the true statements and an "F" in front of the false statements in the spaces provided. If false, explain why.

_____ **1.** In most states, a delinquent is defined as a person under 18 years of age.

_____

_____ **2.** One reason for juvenile crime is a lack of parental supervision and guidance.

_____

_____ **3.** Studies show that high-school dropouts who do not have jobs often become delinquents.

_____

_____ **4.** Drug addicts often turn to crime as a means of supporting their habit.

_____

_____ **5.** Peer pressure does not play a major role in a juvenile's breaking the law.

_____

_____ **6.** A juvenile's guilt or innocence often is determined in a court trial.

_____

_____ **7.** Juveniles have the same rights of due process as adults.

_____

_____ **8.** When a youth is 18 or older and accused of a felony, he or she is tried as an adult in most states.

_____

POST-READING QUICK CHECK After you have finished reading the section, list the various punishments and alternatives for juvenile offenders. Write the pros and cons of these punishments and alternatives. Decide which you think are most likely to bring about positive changes in the life of young offenders.

_____

_____

_____

CHAPTER **17**

Guided Reading Strategies 17.1

The Economic System

READING THE SECTION As you read the section, fill in the blanks with the correct term or terms to complete each statement.

The economic system in the United States is called a(n) _____.

In a(n) _____, buyers and sellers are free to choose, and there

is limited government intervention. People _____ or put

money into a business with hopes of making a(n) _____. In

the American economic system, the laws of _____ and

_____ determine the amount of products businesses provide

and the _____ they charge for their products. Because

Americans can invest _____, or money, in businesses,
our economic system is often referred to as a capitalist system or

_____. Government does protect against unfair business

practices and the formation of _____, when no competition
exists in an industry. Sometimes monopolies are formed when businesses combine to

form a single company, or they _____. Another form of
monopoly occurs when one board of trustees controls several companies, determines
the prices, and makes decisions for all of them. This type of arrangement is known as

a(n) _____. Government has laws to ensure that these large

businesses, or _____, do not abuse their status. It safeguards
against unfair practice with antitrust legislation.

POST-READING QUICK CHECK After you have finished reading the section, write a
story about supply and demand using snow shovels as the product being sold. Imagine
that you own a hardware store in Canton, Ohio. Your story should be written about a
one-year period and should show how you would price the snow shovels.

_____

_____

_____

_____

CHAPTER 17

Guided Reading Strategies 17.2

The Economic System

READING THE SECTION As you read the section, match each of the following terms with the correct definition and place the letter in front of the matching term in the space provided.

_____ **1.** common stock

_____ **2.** corporations

_____ **3.** dividends

_____ **4.** nonprofit organizations

_____ **5.** partnership

_____ **6.** preferred stock

_____ **7.** sole proprietorship

_____ **8.** stockholders

_____ **9.** stocks

a. business owned by one individual

b. shares of ownership in a business

c. less risky shares in a company that receive profits first

d. people who buy shares in a company

e. profits that go to corporate shareholders

f. charities and cultural programs often are examples

g. business owned by two or more individuals

h. riskier shares of corporate ownership

i. licensed by state governments and owned by shareholders

POST-READING QUICK CHECK After you have finished reading the section, write the advantages and disadvantages for each type of business organization. Write the advantages in the first space provided (a) and the disadvantages in the second (b).

1. Sole proprietorship

   a. _____

   b. _____

2. Partnership

   a. _____

   b. _____

3. Corporation

   a. _____

   b. _____

CHAPTER **17** Guided Reading Strategies 17.3

The Economic System

READING THE SECTION As you read the section, fill in the correct information to complete the chart below.

Four Factors of Production	Definition and Example of Each
1.	a.
2.	b.
3.	c.
4.	d.

Write the correct term for each definition in the space provided.

5. Money used to pay for land, buildings, or office space owned by another _____

6. Worker output _____

7. Total amount of money a firm receives from the sale of goods and services _____

8. Amount of money a business has left after expenses have been paid _____

POST-READING QUICK CHECK After you have read the section, write an idea for a business venture that you would like to start. List expenses that you think would be required to run your business.

_____

_____

_____

_____

_____

_____

CHAPTER 18   Guided Reading Strategies 18.1

Goods and Services

READING THE SECTION As you read the section, fill in the blanks by listing the following information.

1. Economic indicators

   a. _____

   b. _____

   c. _____

2. Methods of mass production

   a. _____

   b. _____

   c. _____

3. Industrial power sources (in chronological order)

   a. _____

   b. _____

   c. _____

   d. _____

POST-READING QUICK CHECK After you have finished reading the section, write the name of the person that fits each description in the space provided.

1. I revolutionized the way automobiles were built and made them affordable to the masses.

   Who am I? _____

2. I was able to mass produce guns by making the parts a standard shape and size.

   Who am I? _____

3. I brought affordable lighting to American homes and electricity to factories.

   Who am I? _____

4. I changed the way computers were sold and met consumers' needs at a lower price.

   Who am I? _____

Guided Reading Strategies 18.2

Goods and Services

READING THE SECTION As you read the section, write the letter of the correct definition in the space provided.

_____ **1.** advertising

_____ **2.** brand name

_____ **3.** distribution

_____ **4.** mass marketing

_____ **5.** one-price system

_____ **6.** retailers

_____ **7.** self-service

_____ **8.** standard packaging

_____ **9.** wholesale

a. customers select items and help themselves

b. selling goods in large quantities

c. goods already wrapped from the manufacturer

d. goods sold in large quantities to distributors

e. the means of informing and persuading customers to buy a firm's products

f. a widely advertised and distributed product

g. stores that sell goods directly to the public

h. prices are stamped or printed as barcodes on products

i. the process of moving goods from manufacturers to consumers

POST-READING QUICK CHECK After you have finished reading the section, list the three types of transportation used to distribute goods. Also write the pros and cons of each in the spaces provided.

Types of Transportation Pros (a) and Cons (b)

1. _____

   a. _____

   b. _____

2. _____

   a. _____

   b. _____

3. _____

   a. _____

   b. _____

CHAPTER **18**   Guided Reading Strategies 18.3

Goods and Services

READING THE SECTION As you read the section, write a *T* in the space in front of the true statements and an *F* in front of the false statements. If false, explain why.

_____ **1.** The Nutrition Labeling and Education Act of 1990 requires labels to identify fat and fiber content, serving size, and other nutritional information.

_____

_____ **2.** If you are dissatisfied with a product and feel it was mislabeled or falsely advertised, you should contact the Better Business Bureau first.

_____

_____ **3.** Shoplifting may cause businesses to charge customers higher prices.

_____

_____ **4.** A person using a credit card can often buy a product for a lower price than someone paying with cash.

_____

_____ **5.** Charge account customers who pay their bills regularly establish a good credit rating.

_____

_____ **6.** Installment plans allow customers to buy and use a product with a down payment and pay in installments on the balance.

_____

POST-READING QUICK CHECK After you have finished reading the section, write some attributes that make a person a good shopper and some things to watch out for when using a credit card.

_____

_____

_____

_____

_____

_____

CHAPTER **19** Guided Reading Strategies 19.1
Managing Money

READING THE SECTION As you read the section, fill in the blanks with the correct term to complete each statement.

1. Buyers and sellers use _____ as a medium of exchange.

2. A term used for coins and paper money is _____.

3. A written and signed order to a bank to take money from a person's account is a _____.

4. A(n) _____ is used like a check to deduct money from a person's account.

5. Similar to charge cards, _____ can be used at a variety of stores.

6. _____ are the people or businesses who allow items to be paid for at a later date.

7. Borrowing for a home or vehicle would be examples of _____.

8. _____ is the legal declaration that a person is unable to pay his or her debts.

9. Mints that make coins for general circulation are located in both _____ and _____.

10. Mints that make commemorative coins are located in both _____ and _____ .

POST-READING QUICK CHECK After you have finished reading the section, write a paragraph for a newspaper column on how to avoid bankruptcy and overextending your finances.

_____

_____

_____

_____

_____

Name _____ Class _____ Date _____

Guided Reading Strategies 19.2

Managing Money

READING THE SECTION As you read the section, fill in the missing information to complete the chart on financial institutions.

FINANCIAL INSTITUTION	DESCRIPTION	SPECIALIZATION
1.		
2.		
3.		
4.		

POST-READING QUICK CHECK After you have finished reading the section, answer the following questions in the spaces provided.

1. What are the FDIC, FSLIC, and the NCUA? How are they different?

_____

_____

2. What is the Federal Reserve System? What are its purposes?

_____

_____

CHAPTER 19   Guided Reading Strategies 19.3

Managing Money

READING THE SECTION As you read the section, fill in the blanks with the correct term to complete each sentence.

Most families try to save money for emergencies, education, and major purchases. Two of the most expensive purchases that families make are buying a car and buying a

_____. There are a number of ways to save money. Putting a

regular amount in a _____ or passbook account can earn interest for the depositor, and banks generally require a small minimun balance on this type of

account. Certificates of debt or _____, earn interest from the government when the bond reaches maturity. Stocks are another way to save and can be

purchased over the Internet or from a _____, a person who is employed by a brokerage house. Brokerage houses are members of the

_____. Buying stocks involves more _____ than many other

types of savings. Many people buy _____ because they are less risky than regular stock purchases. When people put a specific amount of money in a financial institution for a certain time period, they are investing in

_____. Like mutual funds, _____ buy stock that is too expensive for most investors to buy individually. Money can be withdrawn from these funds at any time, but this type of investment is not insured by the

_____. Saving money is not necessarily investing money. Investing money involves earning interest. When you invest you are turning your money into

_____, and it is used for expansion in the economy. People want to feel that their money is safe in financial institutions. All banks must receive a

_____ from the state or federal government to operate. All banks

must also obey banking laws and keep reserve funds in the _____ banks.

POST-READING QUICK CHECK After you have finished reading the section, name the agencies that the federal government established during the 1930s to protect depositors and investors. Name the main function of each agency.

_____

_____

_____

CHAPTER **19**

Guided Reading Strategies 19.4

Managing Money

READING THE SECTION As you read the section, match the correct definition with each term by wrtiting the correct letter in the space provided.

_____ **1.** disability income
           insurance

_____ **2.** insurance

_____ **3.** beneficiary

_____ **4.** Medicaid

_____ **5.** Medicare

_____ **6.** policyholder

_____ **7.** private insurance

_____ **8.** social insurance

_____ **9.** Social Security

a. voluntary insurance to cover unexpected losses

b. system of paying a small amount to avoid the risk of heavy insurance loss

c. government medical insurance program that pays costs of low-income people

d. payments to cover lost wages when a person cannot work

e. person named in the policy to receive the money when the policyholder dies

f. government insurance program that gives cash benefits to retired people

g. government programs that are meant to protect citizens from future hardships

h. person who pays insurance premiums for various types of coverage

i. government medical insurance program for older Americans

POST-READING QUICK CHECK After you have finished reading the section, answer the following questions in the spaces provided.

1. How do insurance companies both cover the losses of policyholders and make a profit?

_____

_____

2. What are some of the fraudulent actions that cause policyholders to pay higher premiums?

_____

_____

3. What are the three parts of the Social Security program? How is the program funded?

_____

_____

Name _____ Class _____ Date _____

Economic Challenges

READING THE SECTION As you read the section, match each term with the correct definition by writing the correct letter in the space provided.

_____ **1.** business cycle

_____ **2.** contraction

_____ **3.** costs of production

_____ **4.** depression

_____ **5.** expansion

_____ **6.** inflation

_____ **7.** peak

_____ **8.** recession

_____ **9.** trough

a. period of economic growth

b. severe contraction of the economy

c. highest point of business cycle

d. lowest point of business cycle

e. period of economic slowdown

f. severe trough, very hard economic times

g. the ups and downs of the economy

h. rise in prices

i. includes wages, transportation, rent, raw materials

POST-READING QUICK CHECK After you have finished reading the section, answer the following questions about the economic changes brought about by the Great Depression.

1. When did the Great Depression occur? Name one cause of the Great Depression.

_____

2. What was the name of Franklin Roosevelt's program to deal with the Great Depression?

_____

3. What job program employed young people during the Great Depression?

_____

4. Why was the Social Security system created? What does the program provide?

_____

_____

_____

_____

CHAPTER **20**   Guided Reading Strategies 20.2

Economic Challenges

READING THE SECTION As you read the section, fill in the correct information to complete the main points concerning the economy.

Most serious challenges to the economy:

1. _____

2. _____

3. _____

Causes of economic challenges and problems:

4. _____

5. _____

6. _____

7. _____

8. _____

Government responses to economic challenges:

9. _____

10. _____

11. _____

Consumer and worker responses to economic challenges:

12. _____

13. _____

14. _____

POST-READING QUICK CHECK After you have finished reading the section, think about the ways consumers and workers can aid in economic recovery. Then write a plan for you and your family on doing your part to help with economic challenges in this country.

_____

_____

_____

_____

CHAPTER  **20**

Guided Reading Strategies 20.3

Economic Challenges

READING THE SECTION As you read the section, provide the correct term for each description in the space provided.

1. _____ organizations formed by workers to obtain higher wages and improve working conditions

2. _____ representatives of workers and the employer meet to reach an agreement

3. _____ union members walk off the job because their demands have not been met

4. _____ strike technique used to keep a company from hiring replacement workers

5. _____ techniques used instead of strikes, such as cutting back on productivity

6. _____ list containing names of union members that is used by employers to keep members from being hired

7. _____ employer's method of fighting slowdowns by closing factory doors to workers

8. _____ workers must be union members to be hired

9. _____ workers do not have to belong to the union to be hired

10. _____ qualified workers, union or nonunion, are hired. New workers must join the union to keep their jobs

11. _____ nonunion members must pay union dues

12. _____ only an open shop is legal

13. _____ unions force companies to hire more workers than needed

14. _____ a recommendation made by an expert in a labor dispute

15. _____ a binding decision made by an expert in a labor dispute

POST-READING QUICK CHECK After you have finished reading the section, describe the plight of workers in factories during the 1800s.

_____

_____

Name _____ Class _____ Date _____

The U.S. Economy and the World

READING THE SECTION As you read the section, match each of the following terms with the definition by placing the correct letter in the space provided.

_____ **1.** capital goods

_____ **2.** capital resources

_____ **3.** circular-flow model

_____ **4.** competition

_____ **5.** demand

_____ **6.** human resources

_____ **7.** law of demand

_____ **8.** law of supply

_____ **9.** producer

_____ **10.** shortage

_____ **11.** stock

_____ **12.** supply

_____ **13.** surplus

a. laborers who make goods and services

b. when prices go up and people want less of an item

c. amount of items producers provide at a given price

d. person or company that produces goods and services

e. providing more goods and services when prices go up

f. quantity of item demanded is greater that quantity supplied

g. buildings, machinery, and tools used to produce goods

h. money and other items used to produce goods and services

i. quantity of item supplied is greater than demand for the item

j. exchange of resources, money payments, and products

k. represents ownership in a corporation

l. economic rivalry among businesses selling the same item

m. amount of goods and services people want and will pay for

POST-READING QUICK CHECK After you have finished reading the section, describe the following: traditional economy, command economy, market economy, and mixed economy.

_____

_____

_____

_____

Name _____ Class _____ Date _____

The U.S. Economy and the World

READING THE SECTION As you read the section, determine which of the multiple-choice items is the correct answer for each statement. Put the letter of the appropriate answer in the space provided.

_____ **1.** The ups and downs of the economy over time is called
     a. free enterprise.   **c.** capitalism.
     b. the business cycle.   **d.** economic growth.

_____ **2.** The highest point in the economic cycle is the
     a. trough.   **c.** peak.
     b. expansion.   **d.** contraction.

_____ **3.** The lowest point of the economic cycle is the
     a. trough.   **c.** peak.
     b. expansion.   **d.** contraction.

_____ **4.** When a downturn in the economy is particularly bad, it is called a(n)
     a. recovery.   **c.** expansion.
     b. contraction.   **d.** depression.

_____ **5.** Business investment can promote economic expansion by
     a. buying capital goods.   **c.** improving efficiency.
     b. investing in research.   **d.** all of the above

_____ **6.** To promote economic growth, the government might
     a. raise interest rates.   **c.** lower interest rates.
     b. lay off government workers.   **d.** promote peace.

_____ **7.** Which of the following is NOT a leading indicator that the government relies on to predict the economic future?
     a. building permits   **c.** business orders for consumer goods
     b. stock prices   **d.** birth rates

_____ **8.** Which of the following would give immigrants "permanent resident" status?
     a. a visa   **c.** a green card
     b. a passport   **d.** all of the above

_____ **9.** Which of the following does NOT affect economic growth?
     a. government regulation   **c.** business cycles
     b. current events   **d.** all affect economic growth

POST-READING QUICK CHECK After you have finished reading the section, write a paragraph on how the perceptions and expectations of people and businesses can affect the economy.

Name _____ Class _____ Date _____

READING THE SECTION As you read the section, write the term or phrase that matches each statement in the space provided.

1. A network that enables producers and consumers to participate in the economy

   _____

2. Protecting workers and consumers, pollution controls, and encouraging competition are examples

   _____

3. A tax break that encourages businesses to expand

   _____

4. An increase in government spending can reduce this

   _____

5. Unemployment compensation is an example

   _____

6. When the economy is contracting, and government increases the money supply

   _____

7. When government raises the interest rate to slow economic growth

   _____

8. The buying and selling of government securities

   _____

POST-READING QUICK CHECK After you have finished reading the section, explain how each of the following tools of monetary policy affect the economy.

Open-market operations_____

_____

_____

Discount rate_____

_____

_____

Reserve requirements _____

_____

_____

 CHAPTER **21**

Guided Reading Strategies 21.4

The U.S. Economy and the World

READING THE SECTION As you read the section, complete the following statements by filling in the blanks with the correct term from this section.

Because people and countries _____, international trade is possible. The reliance that people and countries have on each other is called _____. Countries trade for goods and services due to specialization. Countries determine what to specialize in by looking at _____ and _____. This is looking at what products and services the country can produce better than its trading partners and that offer the most profit for the country. In making these economic decisions, all countries must make _____, or economic sacrifices. When a country decides to specialize in one area, the _____ is the value of the area (good and services) that was sacrificed.

Some countries have set up _____ that limit the exchange of goods and services. Taxes that are placed on _____, or goods coming in from other countries, are called _____. Another barrier, _____, limits the amount or number of a certain good or service that can be imported. A(n) _____ completely bans imported goods from a particular country. Trade without any restrictions is called _____. Some countries want restrictions that will give domestic goods an advantage. _____ is using tariffs to protect goods made in the home country.

The income from other countries versus the amount a country spends with other countries is called a country's _____. If a country sells more than it buys, there is a(n) _____. If a country buys more than it sells, there is a(n) _____.

Because there are limited resources and unlimited wants, the problem of _____ exists. Trade can help alleviate this problem because countries can trade for the items they lack. Trade also increases competition among countries and can bring about more efficiency.

POST-READING QUICK CHECK After you have finished reading the section, define the terms absolute advantage and comparative advantage in the spaces provided.

_____

_____

_____

_____

Guided Reading Strategies 22.1

Career Choices

READING THE SECTION As you read the section, decide which statements are true and which are false. Write a *T* in front of the true statements and an *F* in front of the false statements. If false, explain why.

_____ **1.** The freedom to choose your own career is never limited by economic conditions.

_____

_____ **2.** Personal values are not important in determining what occupation to seek.

_____

_____ **3.** A job that offers personal rewards is as important as high pay to many people.

_____

_____ **4.** The least important step in a career decision is getting to know yourself.

_____

_____ **5.** A good education is important in obtaining a high-paying career.

_____

_____ **6.** Employers typically want workers with special training for each position.

_____

_____ **7.** No matter what career path you follow, the best preparation is to learn everything you can in school.

_____

POST-READING QUICK CHECK After you have finished reading the section, make a list of your strengths and your interests. Then make a list of possible career choices that interest you. Which careers match best with your values, interests, and strengths?

_____

_____

_____

_____

_____

CHAPTER 22

Guided Reading Strategies 22.2

Career Choices

READING THE SECTION As you read the section, match each term with the correct definition by writing the correct letter in the space provided.

_____ **1.** agribusiness

_____ **2.** apprenticeship

_____ **3.** automation

_____ **4.** blue-collar workers

_____ **5.** laborers

_____ **6.** operators

_____ **7.** professionals

_____ **8.** service industries

_____ **9.** technicians

_____ **10.** white-collar workers

a. workers that perform manual labor

b. workers such as doctors and teachers who have many years of education and training

c. people who operate machines or equipment

d. workers who perform heavy physical work

e. jobs that require specialized skills

f. businesses that sell services, not products

g. use of machines instead of workers

h. farms run by large corporations

i. people who work in a particular profession who perform technical, managerial, sales, or administrative support work

j. fixed period of on-the-job training

POST-READING QUICK CHECK After you have finished reading the section, answer the following questions about the different types of occupations discussed.

1. What types of jobs (specific) might a person learn by an apprenticeship?

_____

_____

2. Why has the number of blue-collar jobs decreased? Name two reasons.

_____

_____

_____

3. Why do you think women make up approximately 65 percent of workers in the service industry?

_____

_____

_____

Guided Reading Strategies 22.3

Career Choices

READING THE SECTION As you read the section, turn each of the headings in the section into questions using the words who, what, why, when, where, or how. After writing each question, read the information under that heading and then answer the question in the space provided. See the sample question below for government jobs.

1. Government jobs

Question: How can a person apply for a government job?

Answer: _____

2. The armed forces

Question: _____

Answer: _____

3. Workers in demand

Question: _____

Answer: _____

4. Equal opportunity

Question: _____

Answer: _____

5. Unemployment

Question: _____

Answer: _____

POST-READING QUICK CHECK After you have finished reading the section, look back at the list of jobs that should have growth in the next decade. Name reasons why these occupations should grow in the next 10 years.

_____

_____

_____

_____

_____

CHAPTER **22**   Guided Reading Strategies 22.4

Career Choices

READING THE SECTION As you read the section, fill in the missing information in the spaces provided.

1. Name five sources that can be used to find out more about careers.

   a. _____   **d.** _____

   b. _____   **e.** _____

   c. _____

2. Name three things to do when viewing people at work.

   a. _____   **c.** _____

   b. _____

3. Write the seven questions that help evaluate possible careers.

   a. _____   **e.** _____

   b. _____   **f.** _____

   c. _____   **g.** _____

   d. _____

POST-READING QUICK CHECK After you have finished reading the section, write your own answers to the seven questions used to evaluate a career.

   a. _____

   b. _____

   c. _____

   d. _____

   e. _____

   f. _____

   g. _____

Career Choices

READING THE SECTION As you read the section, write the term that fits each description. You may check your answers by unscrambling the term that is provided for each statement.

1. Printed form on which you supply information about yourself.

_____ | lptpncaioia |

2. This tells employers about your grades and the subjects you studied.

_____ | holcso thisyor |

3. A list of these activities tell employers about your potential skills.

_____ | raxelutrciacurr |

4. This information tells whether you prefer indoor or outdoor work, or if you like working alone.

_____ | cipelsa teetnissr |

5. How well, fast, and accurately you use your hands is an indication of this.

_____ | romto lsslik |

6. These determine how well you can visualize or picture things in your mind.

_____ | laurecptpe isklsl |

7. These determine how well you work with others and interact with the public.

_____ | slaortinpeern sliksl |

8. These exams help you explore yourself and assist in discovering your abilities.

_____ | detupati setts |

POST-READING QUICK CHECK After reading the section, use the information about school history, health record, outside activities, and special interests to write a resume for yourself. After you have finished your resume, look at the areas in which you need to improve.

CHAPTER 23   Guided Reading Strategies 23.1

Foreign Policy

READING THE SECTION As you read the section, fill in the blanks with the missing information to complete each statement.

The plans a country has for its interaction with other countries is called

_____. Because of advancements in communication and

transportation, there is more _____ among countries of the

world. The President of the United States is the chief diplomat and is also the

_____ of the U.S. armed forces. The president has the power to

make treaties with foreign countries with the approval of the _____.

Sometimes the president and a foreign leader reach a mutual understanding or

_____ rather than a formal treaty, which would need no further

confirmation. The _____ is appointed by the president and heads

the State Department. This person advises and assists the president and oversees the

_____, which includes all U.S. ambassadors, ministers, consuls,

and their assistants. The cabinet department that informs and advises the president on

military matters is the _____. The secretary of defense and the

president receive military advice and information from the highest officers of the military

branches. Collectively these officers are known as the _____. Other

agencies have been formed by Congress to establish and carry out foreign policy. The

_____ gathers national defense information. The

_____ was created to bring the various leaders together to

coordinate military and foreign policy. Because of the checks and balances built into the

Constitution, Congress also has many powers in U.S. foreign policy. Congress must

confirm presidential treaties with a _____ vote and approve all

cabinet posts.

POST-READING QUICK CHECK After you have finished reading the section, write a paragraph on why it is important for the president and Congress to work together on foreign matters. Use the League of Nations as an example.

_____

_____

_____

Guided Reading Strategies 23.2

Foreign Policy

READING THE SECTION As you read the section, match each of the following terms with the correct definition and place the number of the right answer in the corresponding square in the box below. If the squares all have the correct number placed in them, all the columns and rows will add up to 21.

a. difference in the value of imports and exports

b. meeting between two or more countries on issues of mutual concern

c. goods and services a country sends to other countries

d. trade without barriers or restrictions

e. conducting relations between countries

f. goods a country buys from other countries

g. U.S. volunteer organization that serves in other countries

h. government program that provides economic or military assistance to another country

i. countries that have undergone recent, rapid industrialization

1. free trade

2. European Union

3. Marshall Plan countries

4. NICs

5. exports

6. foreign aid

7. summit

8. diplomacy

9. balance of trade

10. trade deficits

11. Peace Corps

12. imports

a.	b.	c.
d.	e.	f.
g.	h.	i.

POST-READING QUICK CHECK After you have finished reading the section, write the full names and give a brief description for each of the following:

OAS _____

ANZUS _____

NATO _____

EU _____

NAFTA _____

APEC _____

WTO _____

IMF _____

 Guided Reading Strategies 23.3

Foreign Policy

READING THE SECTION As you read the section, fill in the blanks with the correct answer for each of the six divisions of the United Nations.

A. General Assembly

1. _____ number of members

2. _____ vote per member

B. Security Council

3. _____ number of members

4. _____ number of permanent members

5. _____ number needed to pass measure

6. _____ number of permanent members needed to pass a measure

C. International Court of Justice

7. _____ number of judges

8. _____ number of years in term

9. _____ majority needed for court decisions

D. Economic and Social Council

10. _____ number of member countries

11. _____ purpose or mission

E. Trusteeship Council

12. _____ created after this

13. _____ suspended this year

F. Secretariat

14. _____ title of person in charge

15. _____ term of office

16. _____ nominates officials

POST-READING QUICK CHECK After you have read the section, name the five principles of the Atlantic Charter and then name the five permanent members of the UN Security Council.

_____

_____

Guided Reading Strategies 24.1

Charting a Course

READING THE SECTION As you read the section, answer the questions in the blanks provided.

1. What three problems hampered President Washington's policy of isolationism?

_____

2. What were three causes of the War of 1812? _____

_____

3. What did the Rush-Bagot Treaty accomplish? _____

_____

4. Why did President James Monroe issue the Monroe Doctrine?_____

_____

5. How did President Theodore Roosevelt's corollary policy strengthen the Monroe

Doctrine? _____

6. Why did the U.S. policy concerning Latin America become known as dollar diplomacy?

_____

7. How did President Franklin Roosevelt's Good Neighbor Policy improve relations with

Latin America? _____

_____

8. How did U.S. senators indicate their support for isolationism after World War I?

_____

9. What event brought about U.S. involvement in World War II?

_____

POST-READING QUICK CHECK After you have finished reading the section, describe how the United States helped the Allies during World War II before actually entering the war in 1941.

_____

_____

Guided Reading Strategies 24.2

Charting a Course

READING THE SECTION As you read the section, determine which of the following statements are true and which are false. Write *T* in front of the true statements and write *F* in front of the false statements.

_____ **1.** The ideas behind modern communism favored capitalists and industrialists throughout the world.

_____ **2.** Under a communist economic system, the proletariat would control factories and the government.

_____ **3.** The Soviet Union turned Western European countries into satellite nations after World War II.

_____ **4.** The ideas behind the Truman Doctrine came to be known as containment.

_____ **5.** The United States and Britain kept West Berlin supplied by air during the Berlin Blockade.

_____ **6.** After World War II, communists led by Mao Zedong took over Taiwan.

_____ **7.** Because of the balance of power that existed between the United States and Cuba, President Kennedy ordered that long-range missiles be removed from the Soviet Union.

_____ **8.** Because of the Vietnam War, South Vietnam remains free from communism today.

_____ **9.** The policies of glasnost and perestroika were part of Mikhail Gorbachev's reforms in the Soviet Union.

POST-READING QUICK CHECK After you have finished reading the section, explain how the United States got involved in Vietnam without a declaration of war from Congress.

_____

_____

_____

_____

_____

_____

_____

Charting a Course

READING THE SECTION As you read the section, describe the United States' relationship with each of the following countries or regions after the Cold War.

1. Russia and Eastern Europe _____

_____

_____

2. Iraq _____

_____

_____

3. Israel _____

_____

_____

4. India and Pakistan _____

_____

_____

POST-READING QUICK CHECK Match the following leaders (past or present) with the countries or groups they represent(ed).

_____ **1.** Nelson Mandela   **a.** Iraq

_____ **2.** Yasir Arafat   **b.** Israel

                                       c. Colombia

_____ **3.** Saddam Hussein   **d.** Palestinians

_____ **4.** Yitzhak Rabin

                                       e. South Africa

_____ **5.** Andres Pastrana   **f.** al Qaeda

_____ **6.** Osama bin Laden

Guided Reading Strategies 25.1

Improving Life for All Americans

READING THE SECTION As you read the section, turn each of the following terms into questions using the words *who, what, where, when, why,* or *how.* Then answer each question in the space provided.

1. urban development

Question: _____

Answer: _____

2. shrinking cities

Question: _____

Answer: _____

3. urban decay and urban renewal

Question: _____

Answer: _____

4. homelessness

Question: _____

Answer: _____

5. zoning laws

Question: _____

Answer: _____

6. the transportation tangle

Question: _____

Answer: _____

POST-READING QUICK CHECK After you have finished reading the section, fill in the blanks to complete the following statements.

1. Low-rent apartment buildings built with tax funds are called

_____.

2. The rebuilding and revitalization of inner cities is called

_____.

3. Laws that regulate where businesses can locate are called

_____.

CHAPTER 25 Guided Reading Strategies 25.2

Improving Life for All Americans

READING THE SECTION As you read the section, match each of the following terms with the correct definition in the space provided.

_____ **1.** AARP

_____ **2.** ADA

_____ **3.** boycott

_____ **4.** civil disobedience

_____ **5.** civil rights movement

_____ **6.** demonstration

_____ **7.** discrimination

_____ **8.** dissent

_____ **9.** ethnic group

_____ **10.** minority groups

_____ **11.** NAACP

a. groups that do not have as much political and economic power as other groups

b. people of the same race, nationality, or religion

c. group that works on behalf of older Americans

d. to stop using a service in protest

e. act which made it illegal to discriminate against people with disabilities.

f. unfair actions taken against people because they belong to a particular group

g. disagreement or disapproval

h. disobeying laws believed to be unjust

i. mass gathering of dissenters who march and protest

j. group formed to achieve equal rights for African Americans

k. struggle for equal rights for African Americans and other minority groups

POST-READING QUICK CHECK After reading the section, identify and write a sentence about each of the following individuals.

Dr. Martin Luther King Jr.

_____

Mel Martinez

_____

Alberto Gonzalez

_____

Rosa Parks

_____

CHAPTER **25**  Guided Reading Strategies 25.3

Improving Life for All Americans

READING THE SECTION As you read the section, find the correct term or terms to fill in the blanks and complete each statement.

1. A state of physical, mental, and social well-being is _____.

2. The federal department that advises state and local governments on health issues and distributes federal funds is the _____.

3. Dependency on legal or illegal drugs, or _____, can cause life-threatening health problems and societal problems, as users sometimes resort to crime to support their habit.

4. People suffering from _____ not only put their own health and safety at risk but may also jeopardize the well-being of others.

5. Because of the damage that _____ cause in smokers and those who breathe in secondhand smoke, smoking is banned from many public places.

6. Millions of people are infected with HIV, which causes _____, one of the most serious health problems facing the world.

7. Alcohol and excessive speed are two major causes of _____, which cause injury to millions each year.

8. The use of _____ in homes and businesses can provide early warning to people by helping them escape fires.

9. _____ is the key to preventing many accidents, abuses, and the spread of communicable diseases that affect Americans' health and safety.

POST-READING QUICK CHECK After reading the section, write down the most pressing problems affecting the "wellness" of American citizens and one preventative measure for each.

_____

_____

_____

_____

_____

CHAPTER 26   Guided Reading Strategies 26.1

                             The Global Environment

READING THE SECTION As you read the section, fill in the blanks with the correct
answers for each question or statement.

1. Name three typical examples of ecosystems. _____

_____

2. Name three ways that Americans have upset or destroyed the ecosystem.

_____

_____

3. Name three measures that can prevent erosion._____

_____

_____

4. Name two causes of desertification. _____

_____

5. Name two hazards from the use of pesticides. _____

_____

6. Name three ways that the overpopulation of the world strains resources._____

_____

_____

POST-READING QUICK CHECK After you have finished reading the section, write a
paragraph describing the dangers and problems affecting the environment and ecosystem. Then write a paragraph discussing possible remedies or solutions to those
problems and dangers.

_____

_____

_____

_____

_____

CHAPTER  **26**   Guided Reading Strategies 26.2

The Global Environment

READING THE SECTION As you read the section, decide which of the multiple choice items answer each statement correctly, and write the appropriate letter in the space provided.

_____ **1.** Air is an example of
  a. the hydrologic cycle.
  b. the greenhouse effect.
  c. a nonrenewable resource.
  d. a renewable resource.

_____ **2.** Many scientists believe that the increase of carbon dioxide is causing an increase in the Earth's temperature, or
  a. the hydrologic cycle.
  b. a nuclear reaction.
  c. the greenhouse effect.
  d. ozone layer destruction.

_____ **3.** Scientists have discovered that CFCs have caused
  a. hydrologic cycle.
  b. nuclear accidents.
  c. the greenhouse effect.
  d. ozone layer destruction.

_____ **4.** When pollutants mix with water vapor, they cause
  a. acid rain.
  b. ozone layer destruction.
  c. volcanic eruptions.
  d. the greenhouse effect.

_____ **5.** The process that causes precipitation is called
  a. acid rain.
  b. the hydrologic cycle.
  c. volcanic eruptions.
  d. the greenhouse effect.

_____ **6.** Factories and pesticides cause the type of water pollution known as
  a. chemical pollution.
  b. sewage.
  c. thermal pollution.
  d. crud.

_____ **7.** The type of water pollution that can cause cholera, typhoid, and hepatitis is called
  a. chemical.
  b. sewage.
  c. thermal.
  d. silt.

_____ **8.** Landfills can damage
  a. soil.
  b. groundwater.
  c. fishing.
  d. all of the above

POST-READING QUICK CHECK After you have finished reading the section, write down different types of recycling projects, and tell how each would help in preventing pollution.

_____

_____

_____

_____

_____

Name _____ Class _____ Date _____

 Guided Reading Strategies 26.3

The Global Environment

READING THE SECTION As you read the section, write the correct term for each description in the space provided. Check your answers by unscrambling the letters.

1. Resources that can only be used once—like minerals, ores, metals, and fossil fuels—are

_____ | wealbennroen seorruces |

2. Petroleum, natural gas, and coal—which have been formed from the remains of plants and animals over millions of years—are examples of these.

_____ | sifols leufs |

3. Plastics, pesticides, and some chemicals are made from this.

_____ | mruopleet |

4. To keep from depleting natural resources, these types of measures must be used.

_____ | naerocnotivs |

5. Because it is the cleanest-burning fossil fuel, the demand for it has increased in recent years.

_____ | taaruln sag |

6. This is the most plentiful fossil fuel but is one of the most costly to the environment.

_____ | laco |

7. The dangers from the use of this energy source make its use controversial.

_____ | runacle |

8. This alternative source of electricity is generated when water comes in contact with hot underground rocks and turns to steam.

_____ | meeglahtor nergey |

POST-READING QUICK CHECK After you have finished reading the section, list some of the dangers of using nuclear power as an energy source.

_____

_____

_____

CHAPTER **26**

Guided Reading Strategies 26.4

The Global Environment

READING THE SECTION After reading the section, fill in the missing information in the chart below concerning government intervention to save the environment.

Governmental Acts/Laws/Departments	Goals/Outcomes/Significance
1. National Park Service	
2. National Environmental Policy Act	
3. Clean Air Acts	
4. water pollution control acts	
5. Resource Conservation and Recovery Act	
6. Endangered Species Acts	
7. Environmental Protection Agency	

POST-READING QUICK CHECK After reading the section, describe when and why Earth Day was started.

_____

_____

_____

_____

_____

_____

_____

_____